MW00963799

Minimalist Living

*How to Declutter, Spend Less
Money, and Focus on What
Matters*

JAKE ALLEN

Table of Contents

Chapter 1 - An Introduction to Minimalism

Minimalism is a practical route to take that can help you find liberation and freedom. It is a culture that involves getting down to the basics and removing desires and clutter out of life, while making room for more of what's important (dreams, experiences, passion, growth, happiness, and more). More and more people are finding this lifestyle beneficial. In fact, the Japanese have been practicing minimalism for a long time due to the constraints of land and the lack of space in Japan. If you look at Japanese-born brands like MUJI you can already tell that they embrace minimalism as part of their lifestyle.

What kind of freedom would minimalism offer?

- Freedom from fear

- Freedom from worry

- Freedom from feeling too overwhelmed

- Freedom from guilt

- Freedom from depression

- Freedom from consumerism

What is Minimalism?

According to Joshua Fields Millburn & Ryan Nicodemus (the people behind the well-known blog and podcast 'The Minimalists"), minimalism can be defined as "a tool to rid yourself of life's excess for focusing on what's important—so you can find happiness, fulfillment, and freedom."

Minimalism involves getting rid of the superficial materialism. It involves spending less by buying only what you need. It's about focusing on the bare essentials rather than indulging in your desires. By removing the stuff you don't really need, you make room for more meaningful things like relationships, experiences, and passions. And with this shift in what's important, you're able to take action on what you really identify with, rather than let your material possessions define you. Minimalism can be a very personal experience and can mean a variety of things to different people, each with their motives and agenda.

Plenty of individuals in the minimalist movement have pursued this way of life for several reasons. Some do this to consume less, some to focus on health, some to discover their purpose and mission in life, some to pursue their passions, some to eliminate discontentment, and some to contribute to and create more for the society and community around them.

The concept of minimalism is to attain happiness not through material objects but through life itself. And that's all we want in life, isn't it?

Happiness, just like the reasons for minimalism, is very subjective and personal. Different people find happiness in different things. But ultimately, research has shown that there is a stronger connection between happiness and social relationships & experiences over happiness and money & external material possessions.

So really, it is up to us to find what is necessary to feel happy and what is just clutter.

In the next few chapters, we will present to you various ideas on how you can achieve a minimalist lifestyle without adhering to an arbitrary set of rules.

Like everything else, starting out and taking the first steps is always hard but eventually, it'll get easier as you go on, and life will be much more rewarding and fulfilling.

Take note that there is absolutely NOTHING WRONG with material possessions. This movement is for people who want to live a more basic life. Our world today has become extremely consumerist and materialistic that we end up assigning too much meaning to our possessions. In that process, we end up not taking care of our health and relationships, our passions and personal growth. That said, minimalism isn't to say that you cannot own a car or a house or those pair of Manolo Blahniks. There is nothing inherently wrong with owning things. It simply means minimizing the fluff around you so you can make better decisions consciously and more deliberately.

Is minimalism right for you?

Advertisements often make consumers feel like happiness is attached to the purchase of a brand's product or services. The notion is that buying a fashionable shirt will make us cool and beautiful, or purchasing an all terrain SUV will make us go places, or engaging in super fast internet will enable us to enjoy hours and hours of fun.

Does retail therapy make us happy? It could bring us temporary joy, but having it create lasting happiness is another question. If you're feeling unhappiness/depression, retail therapy may act as temporary relief, but unfortunately that sadness will linger until you actually deal with it and take action to resolve it. This is why minimalism is great - it provides a way to create room for the domains that bring us actual joy.

When minimalism is spoken off, many people often think of a barren white wall, a single clothing rack, 2 pairs of shoes, no cars, and empty cupboards.

When this image is conjured, they then decide that it isn't the way to enjoy life. But in reality, being a minimalist is deciding what minimalism means to you and how it fits with your lifestyle.

A minimalist's lifestyle is not identical – everyone on this journey is unique because what you decide to cut out is entirely up to you. It is really about "Determining the most important pursuits in your life, whilst removing everything else that is distracting us from reaching our pursuit." In doing so, you will find other ways to add richness and fulfillment in your life.

Thinking of becoming a minimalist? Here are 10 aspects to consider whether this lifestyle fits you or not:

Do you spend a lot of time cleaning?

If you like clean, organized spaces but do not like

cleaning, minimalism could be for you. The easiest way to reduce clutter and cleaning time is simply to own fewer things. The less stuff you have, the less to clean!

Are you trying to reduce debt/get out of debt?

The thing about debt is that it keeps us in a financial bind and this bind is a huge weight on our shoulders. Obviously, reducing your debts and staying out of it is made easier when you buy fewer things and save more. It's a conscious decision that once made and put into force, is one of the most life-giving actions that you can take.

Do you look forward to a stress-free life?

Who doesn't, right? What we don't realize is that the physical mess around us is a huge reason for extra stress, and the constant desire to buy more things points to the item above that it makes it harder to remove debt. By removing the clutter that surrounds us and the desire for things, we limit the distractions we face, which in turn will help us relax more.

Do you want to maximize your day?

Our belongings drain so much of our time and energy. For example, electronic gadgets like our smartphones take up so much of our time. It's easy to not realize, but each time we feel bored it's common to catch ourselves going through our phones. We're constantly consumed by our things. Our physical clutter requires us to clean more, organize more, maintain, repair, shop, and replenish. Our daily possessions demand a lot of upkeep. Owning fewer items results in less time maintaining them.

Do you want to become more environmentally conscious?

With each product you pick up or coffee you drink or place you drive to, do you find yourself wondering if there's a more environmentally friendly choice you can make? By using fewer resources, minimalism reduces our impact on the environment and the amount of waste we create.

Do you find yourself enjoying being frugal with your money?

Spending less money on physical clutter allows you the freedom of opportunity. Being a minimalist doesn't mean you need or should spend less. It is about making better and higher quality purchases that will last longer.

Do you feel drawn to support causes that benefit the community at large?

Having the opportunity to use money for other causes that you believe in is a big principle of minimalism. These causes can include both your own individual causes as well as the causes you believe in. When you become content with what you have right now, you find yourself having more time to support causes that matter to you.

Do you place a higher value on non-material possessions?

Minimalism allows us to focus on things that we value most - our family, our significant other, our children, and more. Being minimal intentionally promotes the things in life that we value most rather than our things.

Do you feel invigorated by change?

If you are someone that embraces change, chances are you can embrace minimalism as it is a counter-cultural lifestyle. It changes the way you spend, the way you use your energy, the way you save, the choices you make in life, and so on.

Do you often think that life is too valuable to live it the way other people want you to?

If you're answering yes to this question, you might

want to consider minimalism. Your values, your preferences, your ideals, your likes and desires, and your passions are unique to you, and life is too short to live the ideas of other people. Minimalism rejects the general idea that consumerism is necessary, that you need to work most of your life to obtain things you don't need.

Your practice and route of minimalism are also going to be different. There is no clear-cut, a one-size-fits-all method that works for everyone. The fundamental principle of minimalism is to remove all things that are unnecessary in your life and focus on things that you value the most, promote the things that are important to you, and eliminate anything that distracts you.

Chapter 2 - The Benefits of a Minimalistic Lifestyle

It's safe to say that you can immediately see some benefits including a more organized household, less cleaning, less stress, and less money spent unnecessarily. Here is a list of more benefits to consider if you're thinking about switching to a minimalistic lifestyle:

1. Create Room for More Important Things

When we start purging out all unnecessary things

out of our life - whether it be nonphysical or physical, we create space, and we also create tranquility. Think about it. Every time you do a little bit of spring cleaning, don't you feel more relaxed and mentally at peace? Minimalism helps us create opportunities that have a deeper meaning.

2. More Freedom

Accumulating items just because they are attractive or because they make us look/feel a certain way only makes us conform to society's expectations. It also anchors you down. You have less space to move forward financially because the things that you purchase just end up adding to your credit. Not only that, but it also makes it even harder for us to let go. We tend to hold onto things sometimes because we like to wonder if we'll need it in the future. Before you know it, you are becoming a little hoarder.

3. Better Focus

All of us have a passion for something. Many of us

have already found it while some of us are still searching, and many of us don't even know if we have a passion for anything (and that's okay). If you love makeup and you always buy makeup, that doesn't mean that you can't be a minimalist. Similarly, if you like cars or bikes and you're always fixing them or buying parts, it also doesn't mean you can't be a minimalist.

Minimalism creates the opportunity to focus on the things that you love, and it also creates the time for it. The point is, this lifestyle lets you choose what matters less and strip that from your life. If makeup is your passion, but you find yourself buying other items you desire temporarily, you could be wasting time and money putting in effort on things that don't matter. Instead, buy the bare minimum for other things and focus your energy, time, and money on makeup.

4. Less Focus on Material Possessions

Many who buy things may actually be doing it to fill a particular void. For example, some of us think that we need to buy all the latest outfits because otherwise, we won't fit in or look fashionable. We may fill a void to be accepted, to be popular, or just to be seen. The obsession with money should end after the initial desire has been satisfied. The urge to keep buying and buying may lead to a path of emptiness. Placing happiness on external factors never works and won't make anyone happy. While it is easy to succumb to extreme consumerism, it is not impossible to remove yourself from it either. We all enjoy stuff, but there must be a line we draw where we recognize that we don't need all the material goods.

5. Peace of Mind

In reality, a lot of the stress and imbalance we may experience in life is something we put on ourselves. For example, we might constantly think about our future and all the things we desire especially after landing our first job. We immediately think about buying our first car, eating nice meals, and getting the new purse that's hot on the market. While wanting all of these things is not inherently wrong, we generally buy things due to temporary desires over needs. Over time, as our salaries increase, we purchase new cars and other luxurious things. And we end up having loads of stress, and our material possessions hold us down. By simplifying our lives, we enable ourselves to cut ties with additional material attachments and cultivate a calmer and peaceful mind.

6. More Happiness

Decluttering brings joy because you have a better focus on things that matter. You find yourself being more efficient and having more concentration.

7. Less Fear of Failing

We often fear because we have bills to pay. Financial worries tend to be a huge part of stress in our daily lives. By having little collateral, you minimize this fear and focus on prioritizing your energy into passions and dreams.

8. Enhance Confidence

Being a minimalist promotes individuality as well as self-reliance. You feel much more confident by your pursuit of happiness rather than the search for materials.

9. Greater Purpose in Life

If you feel like you aren't serving your purpose on Earth or there is a burning desire that you need to do more than what you are currently doing, then it could help to work towards a minimalist lifestyle so that you can bring a clear sense of purpose back to your life. You will feel much more motivated to do what you want because your focus is clear, the direction is clear, and there's no clutter and confusion.

10. Creating Real Memories

Memories create happiness in life and make life great. When you pass, people will remember your character and how you treated them, rather than the things or titles you have. People will remember the fun times they had with you, the laughs by the campfire, the adrenaline rush of skiing together, and the Easter meal you cooked with them. When you focus on your relationships instead of stuff that doesn't matter, you create lasting memories that make life great.

Chapter 3 - Your Journey to Becoming a Minimalist

What does a minimalist look like? They come in different shapes and sizes - not one way fits all.

For some, pursuing a passion or revolutionary idea is a far greater priority than investing in high-end goods. Take Apple co-founder Steve Jobs who is known for his minimalistic approach. Steve wears kind of clothing almost all the time- a simple shirt, t-shirt or sweater usually in black and jeans. His go-to choice in clothing cuts down the time needed to think about what to wear. Time is channeled into more important decision making. The same thing can be seen in Apple products.

To some, being minimalistic has a lot to do with how they were brought up. Another famous minimalist would be Sarah Jessica Parker. Unlike her character Carrie Bradshaw from Sex and the City, Parker still remembers her humble beginnings of her family of eight living on welfare. Because of this, she continues to live a modest and frugal lifestyle, in a three-story home in Greenwich Village with her husband, Matthew Broderick. They make grounded financial choices for their lifestyle and kids.

Robert Pattinson continued to live in his modest apartment in London even after the success of Twilight. He confesses that he can live without most things. Though he has tons to spend, one of his only splurges include a guitar unlike other celebrities who waste away their earnings.

For some, minimalism on certain aspects of life is about cherishing the moments. Celebrity couple Kristen Bell and Dax Shepard is also famous for the simple civil ceremony in their local courthouse that came up to a total of $142. Bell had confessed to her penny-pinching lifestyle and to being frugal.

Transitioning to Becoming a Minimalist

There are several methods to transition from a materialistically cluttered lifestyle to a minimalist one. While people find different ways of transitioning, here are some of the basics:

1. Start on a day that you have no social obligations

Decluttering isn't just removing or taking away

your physical items. It is also about eliminating toxic relationships, old ideas, and bad habits. So the first step to decluttering is to use a day that you do not have any obligation or chores or tasks. This allows you to focus on the task that you are about to get into.

2. Make a list

By making a list, you can set priorities. A great way to list things out, for example, is to divide items into physical items, relationships, goals, passions, and so on. You don't necessarily need to make all lists in one go, but the first one to work on would be your physical items list. Once you declutter your space, you can then free up your mind.

3. Remove things

A workable rule of thumb is this - if you haven't used an item for over a year- ditch it. If it's in good condition, send it to charity. If it's still in a box, sell it. Places like Fulfillment by Amazon, Swappa, Carousel, Facebook, and Ebay are great online avenues to sell your stuff while getting some money from it.

4. Get rid of duplicate things

How many pairs of sneakers do you need? Do you need those skinny jeans in every color? Part of the minimalistic culture is to exercise needs against wants. You do need a pair of jeans, but you don't necessarily require three pairs of them in varying shades. Get the drift? Again, this depends on your lifestyle. For some people, jeans are the most basic and everyday used item. Therefore they need multiple pairs. Minimalism is a personal preference, and the idea is to rid yourself of things that will only create clutter.

5. Minimize your paper trail

We live in interesting times where more and more companies and organizations are going paperless. Apart from important documents like social security cards, birth certificates, and loan agreements, minimize your trash and pay your bills online. Keep a backup of your files on a cloud drive.

6. Keep your home clutter free

Whether you're transitioning to minimalism or not, keeping your home clutter free helps with maintenance of your house, a clearer mentality and a place that you can relax and unwind.

7. Simplify mealtimes

Food is life! We get it. But that doesn't mean you should hoard food and other items that create a mess in your kitchen and dining space. Meal prep so you can cook and eat healthy meals throughout the week, lessen waste, and make the most out of leftovers.

8. Travel lightly

When you declutter, you'll find yourself traveling lightly too. Prior to minimizing, you would be subjected to too many material belongings. After reducing what you have, it'll make it easier to decide what to travel with and what not to travel with. That smaller weight means more simple and enjoyable holidays. I've traveled with only a carry-on for about one year and it made moving around so much simpler and made me realize how little you need to live a happy, fulfilling life.

9. Simplify your wardrobe

Simplifying your wardrobe doesn't mean you need to throw your fashion sense out the window. Instead, sticking to the basics and the classics will take you a long way. Minimalistic fashion never goes out of style. Look at Victoria Beckham. Sure she's a bonafide fashionista but look closely and she's mainly just sporting the essentials - white blouse, black pumps, skinny pants. The basics. Anna Wintour keeps her hair the same way and usually is seen in a floral sheath dresses. Embracing a minimalist wardrobe helps you get ready faster, be more efficient, and maintain a closet of clothes that you will definitely wear.

10. Downsizing

Downsizing your house is another option in minimizing your life. Consider downsizing your living space if you can. You can save money as well as save time by letting go of living in a larger space. Smaller units are easier for maintenance and requires less electricity, which also cuts down on bills to pay.

11. Keep the 'One in, One out' rule

Practicing minimalism means sticking to a few personal rules such as the one-in-one-out rule. This rule means when you get something new, something old has to go out. This will help you maintain the balance in your home and space and keep it clutter free. It'll also have an impact on your spending habits because you really need to think about whether your next purchase is validated and necessary or if it's not.

Chapter 4 - How to Shop Like A Minimalist

Now that you've de-cluttered your space and scaled down on your possessions, the hardest part is yet to come.

Maintaining the balance

Maintaining that minimalism culture is harder than reorganizing and removing your clutter but it is achievable if you change your mindset. Shifting your mindset is the first stepping stone towards a different you, no matter what aspect you are working on, whether it is your career, your goals, your lifestyle, your fitness, family life, or relationships. Adjusting the mindset is what we all need to work on if we plan on changing things around us.

For example, if you find your health declining or your weight increasing, the only way you can get healthy and fit and maintain a good weight is by exercising and eating right. You can sign up for classes, get a gym membership, and attempt to cook healthy meals. But without self-realization and a change in mindset, you are bound to fail within the first few days or weeks of your attempted change. However, if you've programmed your mind towards it, then you will succeed. Like the saying goes - it is all in the mind. You'll be focused on a healthier you and you'll take baby steps to create a habit of adjusting your lifestyle by persistence and shifting of perspective. Rather than dread the activities that are required to become healthy and fit, you'll adjust your mind to want those things so that it becomes pleasurable.

Back to the topic at hand. So, after de-cluttering, organizing, creating goals and lists, how do you attempt to stay minimal? It starts with your shopping etiquette.

You need to SHOP like a MINIMALIST.

Below is a series of steps to take when you go shopping. Over time, you will find that this practice will become second nature to you.

1. Plan Ahead

Before shopping, plan what it is that you want to buy. Planning ahead helps you stay on track, and it helps you identify what you need to purchase. After you've tracked what you need, you'll go only into the shops or stores that sell these items you want when you walk into the mall. This prevents you from mindlessly waltzing into stores that don't supply what's on your list. Plan ahead on everything from groceries to makeup, shoes to clothes, and painting materials to kitchenware. Put this into practice and it'll become second nature to enter only stores that you need to enter and grab only things you need.

2. Do your research

Pinterest is a great place to research things related to your purchasing plans. Minimalists often create capsule wardrobes of essential pieces and must-haves, and you can build your own wardrobe by sorting your current stash into LOVE/MAYBE/NOPE or DONATE. Once you're done, look to see what is left and then choose a color palette. Stick to this and accessorize with your remaining shoes, bags, and jewelry. The point is to maximize your options and mix and match so you can use each clothing item in various ways and never run out of style. Research purchases of different items so you know how much each item costs and whether you can afford them.

3. Setting a budget

Once you have an idea of how much your essentials would cost you, it's time to set your budget. Think carefully on how much you can spend and set a clear budget. Stick to it when you go shopping. What you don't want to do is incur more debt onto your credit card for a new pair of shoes that you did not include into your shopping list. Spend only on what you can afford.

4. Source quality items

Your capsule wardrobe, capsule kitchen, or minimalist living room can go a long, long way provided you use your money wisely in making purchases that emphasize quality over quantity. Quality item purchases reduce the need to replace that item in the near future. Quality products will last for years and are more robust and sturdy so you are actually saving money in the long run. Look out for quality items like furniture, kitchenware,

tableware, glassware and certain clothing items
such as jeans and shoes.

5. Ask yourself if it's necessary

We all give ourselves this pep talk when purchasing
something. We ask ourselves if it's worth it, if we
need it, if it's necessary, etc. - and rightly so. Think
about your purchase, if it will add real physical
value. Sure, buying the product may make you feel
good, but the positive emotional impact will only be
temporary. If it is not a necessary item, you'll find
that you won't really use it all that often. So when
buying something, think about how it will add value
or improve your life or even simplify it. If you
already have something similar at home which
works perfectly fine, then don't buy it. There is no
point in having two of the same items when in fact,
you only need one (unless of course you are
replacing something broken).

We can all practice some form of minimalism in our
lives. If your objective is to cut down on

materialism and clutter no matter what your earning power is, then a minimalistic approach to purchasing is what you need in life whether it is to save money, reduce waste, simplify your life, or focus on other goals and passions. It is great for whatever your objectives are. It doesn't hurt to reduce your carbon footprints at the end of the day either, as it will benefit both you and the environment we live in.

Chapter 5 - Simplifying Your Finances

As you begin your journey into minimalism, you will start to feel and experience the benefits of living a simpler life and owning less. Practicing minimalism also has its effect on your finances.

If you think about it, your financial situation is a huge focal point in your life. We become too controlled by it that everything we do revolves around money, and not to mention with the rapid changes in our lives, finances become even more and more complicated.

Here are some steps to help you simplify your financial life and increase your sense of control over it.

1. Get rid of the paperwork

An average working adult has a minimum of two financial accounts, and as we grow older, we end up opening other accounts for the various financial pursuits in our lives. This leads to even more paperwork and bills in our mailbox. Most of the time, we don't know what these numbers mean, or we barely take the time to read them through. The existence of this pile of paperwork is in itself stressful. Whenever you can, shift the paperwork to an online account where you can manage and check your accounts all in one place.

2. Consolidate your accounts

If you have various checking accounts and savings account, it's time to think about consolidating them into one checking account and one savings account. This will not only reduce the paperwork you'd have to deal with but it will also simplify your banking activities.

The same goes for retirement accounts. Simplify your life by transferring all your 401(k) plans into a single self-directed IRA account. This will also help reduce accounting fees and make it easier to manage your retirement assets.

3. Cutting back on your credit cards

The bane of all financial problems starts when we begin with our credit cards. Just like your bank accounts, keep your credit card focus on only one card. Yes, having a credit card is useful for any emergency purposes, but rather than have multiple, choose one card that you feel gives you the best benefits and rewards and cut the rest. Besides, when you start simplifying your life and your purchases, you'd find lesser need to have multiple cards anyway.

4. Pursue a Debt Free Life

Being debt free is one of the ultimate goals of adulthood. Debt costs you money, and it also makes life complicated and bonded. Having multiple debts is a serious reason for stress. Each debt that you acquire increases the complications in your life. Each debt that you remove reduces the complexity. Work towards becoming debt free. While this won't happen overnight, it would help if you establish a plan to lessen the amount of loans you have.

5. Invest wisely

Investing in a smart way helps minimize issues and complications. If you are planning on investing, invest in funds rather than on individual stocks (unless stock investing comes second nature to you and you've studied it a lot). Individual stocks, while fun and rewarding, can be extremely messy to deal with. You would need to research, track, buy and sell each stock in your investment portfolio. And the more you have, the more dedication you need to have when it comes to managing your portfolio. Instead, invest in exchange-traded funds or mutual funds.

6. Reduce your services

If Steve Jobs can simplify his life, you can too. You don't need subscriptions to so many services. Like de-cluttering your closet, if you have not used certain subscriptions for a year- toss it out. This may include magazine subscriptions, music streaming subscriptions, and more. This simplifies your life, it removes another payment element, and it simplifies your finances.

7. Prioritize your goals

Having goals makes us look forward to a fruitful life, gives us challenges, and enables us to achieve significant milestones in our life. Unless you're an expert, don't fuss over trying to achieve multiple goals at one time. Prioritize your goals so that you can focus your energy and time efficiently. Your chances of succeeding are much higher when you prioritize.

9. Focus more on what element brings you the most income

This tip is especially for the self-employed and for people working on commission, but even salaried employees can also benefit from this step. The whole idea is to focus your time and effort on the activities that will likely generate income for you while reduce the time you spend on doing other activities as a result. Think of activities that will bring you a larger bonus, put you in a better position to close a deal or be promoted, and place you on a faster track to success. All these efforts will no doubt simplify the process of attaining your goals and generating the income that you desire.

10. Reduce mental clutter

Yes, there is such a thing as mental clutter and it's all thanks to the gadgets we have on our hands, in front of our faces and our living rooms from our smartphones to iPads and television. With the internet, there is a constant need to keep updating and informing ourselves. However, this may just bring in more confusion. And uncertainty doesn't help in the process of simplifying our financial lives. Limit TV time to one hour after work and do not spend time on your smartphones for at least 30 minutes before bed. Small changes like this bring in a significant impact.

The bottom line is, all these various tips are great strategies that you can use to reduce clutter and make your life more meaningful. Financial clutter only increases stress in our lives.

These strategies and methods explained above can be used by anyone regardless of whether they want to be a minimalist or not. Eliminating stressful components in our life is essential to any human being for a more peaceful and mindful existence.

Chapter 6 - How to Budget Like a Minimalist

In this chapter, we will look into how to manage your expenses. By now, you should know that minimalists like to keep it simple.

But regardless of your income, the rule is always to spend less than what you make otherwise you'd go into debt. As easy as this sounds, many of us, unfortunately, spend more than what we make.

But whether you like it or not, and no matter what your spending power is, never go beyond it. Those with a higher salary may be able to afford more, but even then it is important to keep track and manage your finances well or you'll end up in major debt, or worse, bankruptcy. Certain apps like Mint or Personal Capital are great for tracking your net worth and seeing where your spending is going.

All this seems like it is common sense. However, tons of people are still making these mistakes to this day. So no matter how much you make, you'll always be running into debt regardless of your lifestyle choices if you do not fix this part of your way of life. You need to figure out how much money you need to survive and then realize that everything else beyond that point is just a want and not a need.

What are your resources?

Some people are probably stuck in a full-time 9 to 5 job we don't like. If you do like your job and if your career goals match your passions, then good for you! Regardless of our career choices and circumstances, coming out of a financial rut and living paycheck to paycheck is a goal that you need to achieve.

Think about what your resources are and work towards:

- Getting out of debt

- Creating a budget

- Planning for your future and retirement

- Regaining control of your finances

Think of what your income resources are and how you can use it to save, settle your debts, and plan your future. Again, these things don't happen overnight. It requires planning, sacrifice, discipline, and time.

What are your expenses?

All of us have absolute expenses. These types of expenses are things that you must pay off to live the current lifestyle you have chosen. These absolute expenses may include:

- Rent or mortgage

- Homeowner's Insurance

- Utilities

- Car Insurance

- Gasoline

- Food

- Cellphone

- Health Insurance & Medical Expenses

Health insurance is essential, especially with the rising medical costs year after year. Many companies already offer health insurance but if you are planning to leave your job or you have your own profitable business, you'll need to get yourself your health insurance externally. For people not working in the corporate world, here are some options to follow:

- Purchase a high-deductible policy

- Check prices with the Freelancer's Union

- Compare quotes with an insurance broker

- Get insurance through your spouse's employer

Your expense types may vary. Jot them down so you know what items you need to settle off on a monthly basis. Open your spreadsheet and input the numbers in yourself. These are the necessary expenses for your monthly living.

Another monthly "expense" may be emergency funds for rainy days that you want to set aside in your savings account. From your resources and income, set aside some savings and do not touch it.

You also need to have at least 6 months of your monthly income saved for your basic living expenses.

What kind of expenses can you eliminate?

Things like movies, concerts, date nights, and whatnot are what you can live without. These things are optional so if you do not have the money to do them, don't. Besides, there are plenty of ways to enjoy some leisure time without spending money.

When you look at your list of expenditures, is there anything in there that you can remove? Here are a few examples of certain luxuries that we accumulate not because we need them, but because they're desired.

Expenses you could eliminate:

-       Cable TV (there are plenty of online avenues

you can watch series & movies on for free)

-      The Internet (hotspot your mobile internet so you're paying for only one internet bill)

-      Cleaning Service (you can clean your downsized apartment on your own)

-      New clothes every month (remember - capsule closet)

-      Credit card #1

-      Credit card #2

-      Morning coffees

-      Gym Membership (there are plenty of bodyweight workouts you can try such as calisthenics)

-      Eating out at fancy restaurants

-      New gadgets and other miscellaneous items

This isn't to say you have to cut off all of these things. For example, it could be quite cumbersome to depend on mobile hotspot all the time versus having wireless internet. Or if morning coffees make your day that much better, it could be beneficial to keep it in. Again, it's a matter of figuring out what classifies as a "want" versus a "need" as well as understanding what you value, so you can figure out what you would like to keep in your life or discard.

Question ALL of your purchases

It takes time to earn your money and your time is your freedom. Don't become a slave to your money. By giving up your money for a pair of sunglasses here or a fancy dinner there or a brand new sweater, you are giving up small pieces of your freedom.

So the next time you make a purchase, no matter how small, ask yourself - is this worth my freedom? This kind of thinking can significantly change the way you spend, save, and manage your money.

What is your income?

After questioning your purchases and examining how much money you're spending, you'll be able to figure out exactly how much you would need for your necessities. And if you're working a job that you may not enjoy, you can see how you can merge passion with career while still covering your monthly expenses.

First, you have to figure out what your passions are.

Finding your passion

Some of you already know what it is you like (sleeping is not a passion!) whereas some of us are still out there looking.

What is your passion? Baking? Racing? Sewing? Craft? Video production? Deejaying? Writing? Teaching? Hiking? Fitness?

My best advice is to try all different things and put yourself out there until you find certain activities resonating. If you are passionate about something, you have the option to turn it into a profitable business. It is easy to think that your passion is not monetizable, but with the internet and today's technology, so many opportunities are opened to start your own business.

Identify your mission

For many of us, our mission in life is the same as achieving our passions, but some people's passions and missions are two separate things altogether. Generally, it's said that a great life purpose boils down to two things: 1) personal growth 2) contributing to others. The meaning of life is to not only grow as an individual but also to contribute to the people around you in a meaningful way. You are the person who gets to decide how you plan on doing both.

You're probably wondering what passions and missions have anything to do with being a minimalist.

Nelson Mandela quoted "There is no passion to be found playing small—in settling for a life that is less than the one you are capable of living."

Owning less, making life simpler, focusing on your passions, and figuring out what inspires/motivates us is an excellent roadmap for the life that you've always dreamed of living.

When thinking of the word "blissful", you might think of simple pleasures like:

Sitting on a couch cozy and snug with the love of your life, sipping coffee

Lying down on a hammock, the sun in your face,

reading a book

Enjoying a cup of coffee when it is raining outside

Having ice cream while watching your kids frolic on the beach

All of these are simple pleasures which tell us that our inner self craves of things like this. Though they may be simple, they're difficult to enjoy because we're always in a rush to do something or go somewhere.

But once we discover our mission in life and our passions, we liberate ourselves. We liberate ourselves because that's when we intentionally take effort in changing the way we do things, the way we live our lives, the way we think and the way we respond to our entire ecosystem.

With a solid sense of your life purpose you won't

need to purchase things to live up to other people's ideas of what you should have or be. You feel content with the way things are rather than create an untruthful facade. You appreciate the things you have and are content because your life is meaningful, and you won't need luxuries to feel accepted.

Best minimalist budgeting apps

Once you have figured out what you can live with and without and what kind of income you need to sustain your current lifestyle, it's time to put things in perspective.

For many of us, spreadsheets work great to keep track of your budgets and finances. However, to enhance your budgeting prowess, you can also get your hands on some really cool apps.

Here are some great apps that are free or have minimum charges:

"Daily Budget" App

Daily Budget allows you to calculate not just today's allowance, but the next two days as well. If you have money left over at the end of the day, the app adjusts your check and balance for tomorrow's allowance, which gives you the option for a little more spend and vice versa. This app does not track multiple budgets, but it has a cool feature called 'Big Spendings' which enables you to add a future large purchase or expense. It will then start 'saving' for that expenditure immediately by deducting a percentage of your daily allowance- which you then need to physically remind yourself to do. The app has a very minimalistic interface that is user-friendly and straightforward.

"Digit" App

Digit is a fully automated app great for helping you manage your savings. Every few days, the app automatically transfers cash into your Digit account, and when you do need the money, Digit transfers it back within one day. This hands-off approach is less stressful and helps with building your savings quietly in the background. The app is ideal for people who have a problem stashing away cash from every paycheck into a savings account. You need to connect your bank account to the app and Digit will analyze your spending patterns and locate areas in which cash can be saved.

"Smart Budget" App

Smart Budget is a great app to use for tracking your expenses. It is excellent for people with joint finances and useful if you want to easily get a snapshot of your spending on a daily/weekly basis. However, the Smart Budget app doesn't have a feature to set limits and doesn't feature budgets over multiple accounts.

Summary

There are plenty of financial management apps that are either free or paid that you can try out.

Ultimately, you should try and pick one (or two at the most) that you find fits your needs and your spending lifestyle. Picking too many apps defeats the purpose of a minimalistic approach and can be confusing!

But whether you are using a spreadsheet or an app, your goal should be to simplify your finances and streamline your personal money management because this would be the non-physical aspect of minimizing your life. De-cluttering your bank accounts and finances will mentally lead you towards simplifying your life and reducing the strains we have on our minds and connections to material objects.

Chapter 7 - Minimalist Hacks

Everybody loves a good strategy or "hack" right? It makes things a lot simpler. Smart hacks simplify our lives, which can prove useful in the early stages of your transitioning journey.

Here are some hacks that you can try to make your life easier while on your path to minimalism.

1. Toss - do not store!

Reorganizing your space, your life, and all the little details that wear you down means that in a few months time, you'd be rearranging again. Instead of doing that, toss things out. If you have not used certain items for the past six months to 1 year, it is time to say goodbye to those possessions.

2. Don't go bargain hunting

Bargain hunting only means you'd end up bringing home more stuff. And a lot of times, you buy it not because you need it, but because you don't want to pass up a good deal. This is not what minimalism is about. Just because something is cute and on sale doesn't mean you should get it!

3. Smart small with minimizing!

Starting small is always good. Instead of purging out and decluttering everything in one weekend, start smaller. Try opening a drawer or a cabinet, getting a box, and removing items one by one.

4. Look into the future

Picture yourself with a potential purchase six months down the road. Do you need it? Is the item something you would need after six months? If it's a no, chances are you shouldn't buy it.

5. Do it now, not later

If you feel a space is too cluttered, your workstation needs to be reorganized, or you have plenty of clothes you don't need, get rid of them immediately. Pack up your possessions and get them to a shelter, charity or the garbage.

6. Borrow, don't buy

If there's a need to get something for a one-time occasion- borrow it rather than buy it. If you are planning a party or wedding event for example, there are plenty of sites that provide rental-based party needs from decoration to chairs, trays and the like. There's also plenty of online fashion outlets that specialize in borrowing items for certain fees.

7. Go from paperwork to online documents

As much as you can, minimize paper trail by doing things like finances, paperwork, billing, data keeping and so on in your computer or cloud drives. Scan your documents, your photos, and place them all on your computer & cloud drive.

Chapter 8 - Meaningful Relationships

You now understand how to declutter, organize, budget, and shop like a minimalist. But minimalism also entails focusing on what matters in other areas, including your relationships, passions, and more. In this chapter we will focus on how to create meaningful relationships and cut out people who are pulling you down.

A lot of friendships/relationships are created

because of proximity. You make friends who are close in location with you because it is easiest. But many relationships that are formed only due to distance are doomed to fail. In my own experience, I have had to cut out friendships because I realized we didn't share any common values or beliefs. In fact there were no strong foundations with those friendships. This doesn't mean that I have to have friends who agree with me on everything, but it's hard to grow with people who are moving in opposite directions as I. Rather, it's much easier to interact with people who understand you.

What to look for in a relationship

Relationships should not be fundamentally based on convenience. With friends and loved ones you should generally look for the following:

-People who add value

-People who support you

-People who will do things for you and vice versa

-People who don't victimize themselves

-People who help us grow

-People who share some core aspects with you like values or beliefs

How to handle relationships that don't make sense

With this guide you can kind of understand who makes sense in your life and who doesn't. Surround yourself with people who improve your life and make sense. I try to gravitate away from or cut out people who pull me down.

But it isn't always easy to just stop talking to certain people.

Before you let go of a negative relationship, you can

try to fix the relationship first. You should address why your friend or loved one is draining you and how they could change for the relationship to work. For example, you might need them to be more supportive or you might want them to talk about different topics than the ones they normally do. By letting your friend know how he or she can improve you are taking a step to fixing the relationship. And next you should do the same for them and ask them what they'd like to change about the relationship and how you can improve.

If you can't fix the relationship, it is important let go of someone who is only draining your life. Tell them and move on.

Lastly it is important to maintain the foundationally strong relationships. Do your part by being consistent with your actions, showing how much you care about the person, and helping the other person grow if the person helps you mutually.

Chapter 9 - Setting Goals and Creating Habits

Minimalism is a lifestyle, just like how fitness or dance is a way of life. When you say something is your lifestyle, you are affirming and committing to it. You want to make a change, and you work towards this change by altering the way you think, changing the things you do daily, and working on a routine or schedule to keep you disciplined and on track.

In this chapter, we look at making a personal commitment to ourselves, how to set goals and create habits that will help get us into the habit of minimalism.

Building A Personal Commitment

One of the first few things anyone must do to become a minimalist is to commit and continue practicing this culture.

Your commitment should be that from this day forward, you are going to do the things you know you must do, when you must do them. This commitment must include the rule that you cannot allow yourself to make excuses or justify why you aren't doing what you are supposed to be doing.

It's difficult but the key is to start small. It's the process, not the result. Doing small changes in your daily life will help you towards becoming self-disciplined.

Start your day by waking up early. If your regular wake-up time is at 8 am, then make it 7.30am. Make your bed and empty out the trash. All these tiny things are what get you en route to becoming more disciplined in your journey to minimalism.

Robert Collier wisely said 'Success is the sum of small efforts, repeated day in day out.'

Building Your Personal Commitment to Change

Commitment is all about taking action to bring out the desired result. Commitment is not a result of an external force; rather, commitment is an internally motivated feature. You need to be willing to take action because you care about the results. So how do you know the strength of your commitment to your professional or personal goals?

All of us create commitments about things and issue that we care about. For instance, you may currently feel discomfort about how things are and start to yearn for something better. You may also be moved by an exciting challenge to create something new for yourself or your company. These are desires that revolve around self improvement and getting to the core of what really matters in your life. So ask yourself - what is it that is important to me and why do I need to change? What are the things I care most about?

Change will never be achieved without any commitment. We need to have a strong commitment that engages us to change and to sustain.

Take Action to Build Commitment for Change

Follow these guidelines to help you make a strong commitment to change:

1. Express and Demonstrate Change

Whether your commitment is to your organization, your job, or your family, always remember that change starts with individuals. Leaders need to be involved in expressing and demonstrating their commitment to goals. Surround yourself with people with this energy as well as create change within yourself. An environment of change needs to be created to encourage others to commit.

2. Be clear on your purpose to change

To make a change is to have a clear focus. If your agenda is clear with measurable results, you will not lose sight of your goals.

3. Invite reflection

Reflecting on what you have done and how you have worked before to attain your previous goals will help you achieve your future ones. Sometimes looking back helps you pinpoint exactly what went wrong and how best to improve on mistakes.

4. Make room for emotional change

Allow yourself to express discomfort, excitement, fear or sadness. You are after all human and making adjustments is a big thing in anyone's lives. You will be experiencing different emotions while attempting a new minimalistic lifestyle change.

5. Be free to commit

Don't restrict yourself when it comes to transitioning/adjusting. Just understand that change takes time and energy so don't expect to succeed in vastly improving yourself at one go and committing immediately. Be patient and keep persisting.

6. Follow through

When you have committed yourself to change, you need to make sure that you clearly demonstrate the actions that are required to make that change. Start small and keep the momentum going until you reach your personal best. After you reach a point, keep reinventing and making new changes. Keep the wheel going and never stop improving.

7 Tricks to Achieve Your Goals like a Pro

Goal setting is different for different people, just like how minimalism is. There are many different pieces of advice on how to do goal-setting right as a minimalist. So in this chapter, we will explore not so much about how to set goals, but more on how to accomplish these goals. Our mind and our subconscious are set up to help us achieve goals that we sincerely believe are achievable. Here are some tricks that can assist you in goal setting and goal getting:

Be A Dreamer, but Stay Motivated

Goals are materialized because each and every one

of us is a dreamer. But to accomplish your goals, you need to do something about them, and that takes self-discipline and motivation.

Your first trick is a mind trick. Have a burning desire and a reason to achieve it. The path to achieving goals is filled with many obstacles like boredom, demotivation, procrastination, anxiety, difficulty, and ultimately, excuses. There will be so many times that you will try to talk yourself out of goals. But to keep going, always remember the reason and the desire of why you wanted to attain this goal as this helps you stay on track.

Break it down

Break down your goals into mini-goals. Your brain probably knows you can't achieve enormous goals in an unrealistic timeline. So when you create your goals, give it a 24-hour cycle. Essentially, create mini goals. For example, if your goal is to eat healthily- don't tell yourself "I'm going on a 30-day gluten-free diet starting today!". This sets you up for failure. Instead of saying 30 days, tell yourself you will go for a three-day gluten free diet and move up from there. Your mini goals must be reasonable, sustainable, and attainable within your 24-hour period.

The more you work on your habits and create a routine, the closer you are to achieving your goals. The first 30 days of a goal is crucial as it boosts your morale, creates a habit, and proves you're serious about what you're doing.

Learn to adapt and adjust

As you continue achieving your mini goals and working towards your bigger goals, be flexible. Be willing to adapt to changes along the way. Make your mini goals slightly difficult if you deem them comfortable. Or if they become too taxing, then make them easier. The main thing is if your goals are too difficult, you might end up quitting, and if they're too easy, then you aren't pushing yourself. Find a middle ground that is decent for advancement each day - so be flexible with the goals you create. As a fitness example, if you have set your mini goal to do 30 push-ups daily and after two weeks in your training you feel you can do more, challenge yourself and bring up the daily goal to doing 40 pushups daily. When it comes to clutter, if you decide removing an item a day is easy, challenge yourself to 2 items daily instead.

Look back for feedback, look forward to rewarding

Feedback and reward are essential parts of goal-setting and goal getting. On your journey to goal-getting, be bold to request feedback from the people around, especially from the ones you look up to. Give yourself a little reward daily or once a week for accomplishing your goals. Rewarding yourself can be simple as putting a gold star on your calendar on the days you've achieved your goals or something more elaborate like a dinner on a Saturday night. This reward giving is positive reinforcement. These little things are good enough to tell your brain that you are doing something right.

Conclusion

Minimalism is not just about downsizing. It is about focusing on what matters in all parts of your life and cutting out things that are unnecessary. It is about spending less money and spending more time with loved ones. It's about finding what you love and doing those things over things you don't care about. It's about bringing in the people who matter most in your life and cutting out the people who only bring negativity.

You should now have a good understanding of what minimalism is and be able to transition into this journey of living a simpler yet fulfilling life. It may seem daunting to live with so little but once you get your foot in the door, you will be able to experience the benefits of minimalism in a very short time.

Again, minimalism is very different for a lot of people but the ultimate goal is to free up space and focus on what you prioritize in life like your passions, your career, your family, and your goals. Whatever your needs and desires are, minimalism helps by removing the clutter out from your life and your mind so you'd have a straight road towards attaining your goals and mission in life.

Made in the USA
Lexington, KY
11 December 2017